GRANDPA'S FAMOUS STORIES

by

Dr. Cedrick Gilbert

PITTSBURGH, PENNSYLVANIA 15238

RoseDog Books
585 Alpha Drive, Suite 103
Pittsburgh, PA 15238
Visit our website at *www.rosedogbookstore.com*

ISBN: 979-8-88527-549-1
eISBN: 979-8-88527-599-6

One rainy Saturday afternoon in Sacramento, California, Little Joseph and his grandfather, gathered around the kitchen table for an afternoon snack. Little Joseph knew his grandfather loved to eat four chocolate chip cookies, a turkey sandwich, and a cool glass of raspberry lemonade during his afternoon snack time. The afternoon turkey sandwich would always consist of wheat bread with mayo on one side, and honey mustard on the other, fresh lettuce and tomatoes, two sprinkles of salt, three sprinkles of pepper, and grandpa's favorite, Swiss cheese. Grandpa never made a turkey sandwich without Swiss cheese!

1

While Little Joseph and his grandfather were enjoying their afternoon snack, Grandpa said, "Little Joseph, I've decided to sell my house, boat, and tire company and move to Atlanta." But Grandpa, Joseph replied, you love your boat and you also promised that one day, I would own and operate the tire company! I don't understand Grandpa, you've lived in California for over sixty years, why on earth would you want to sell everything and move, especially to Atlanta? You know, you are right indeed my boy! I've lived in California for over sixty years and I do love my boat, and that's why it's time for me to do something new and adventurous, like move far, far, away to a new city, meet new people, and experience new things. Grandpa, are you absolutely sure about meeting new people, and experiencing new things, asked Little Joseph? I'm one hundred percent sure, said Grandpa. But Grandpa, what about the tire company you promised I'd own one day?

2

Well Little Joseph, here is the deal, as soon as you graduate from college, I'll start a brand new tire shop in Atlanta, and we will name it Joseph's Tire & Tread Company. Okay Grandpa, that sounds terrific! Grandpa, how far away is Atlanta? I'm not really sure, said Grandpa, but I think Atlanta is over twenty-four hundred miles east of Sacramento. Wow! That's really far, far, away exclaimed little Joseph. What about school Grandpa, do you know anything about the schools in Atlanta, and what school would I attend? I don't know anything about the schools in Atlanta, said Grandpa, but I do know a great deal about the famous people in which the schools in Atlanta are named. Follow me into the family room and I'll tell you a story about some of those famous people.

3

As Grandpa and Little Joseph walked into the family room, Grandpa continued to eat his afternoon snack that always consisted of a turkey sandwich on wheat bread with mayo on one side, and honey mustard on the other side, fresh lettuce and tomatoes, two sprinkles of salt, three sprinkles of pepper, and Grandpa's favorite Swiss cheese. Oh I almost forgot Grandpa's four chocolate chip cookies and his cool glass of raspberry lemonade. Once Grandpa put his food on the table, he turned off the television and sat down in his old squeaky rocking chair.

As Grandpa began to tell the stories of the famous people in which the schools in Atlanta are named, he reached out his hand and gestured for Little Joseph to come sit on his lap. While sitting on Grandpa's lap, Little Joseph began to gaze in Grandpa's eyes in anticipation. Grandpa was the best storyteller in all of California. He would often tell stories about his life experiences. He would also tell funny, sad, and scary stories too. Hearing Grandpa tell stories was always fun and exciting for Little Joseph. Before Grandpa would tell his amazing stories, he would always clear his throat, gulp down three gulps of his raspberry lemonade, and clear his throat once more. Sometimes Grandpa would forget to clear his throat and Little Joseph would have to remind him. When Little Joseph reminded Grandpa to clear his throat, Grandpa would always say, "Oh, I almost forgot, unh-unh!"

But this time, Little Joseph was really anxious to hear Grandpa's story of the famous people because he never heard this story before. However, Grandpa was taking an unusually long time starting. He just stared up at the ceiling. After some time had passed, Little Joseph asked, Grandpa, what's wrong, are you okay? Grandpa continued to stare up at the ceiling, not saying anything. Finally, Grandpa cleared his throat and started to speak. Grandpa would always start his exciting stories with four words, Once Upon a Time! Only this time, he started the story with a question.

Grandpa asked Little Joseph, have you ever heard of a gentleman named Booker T. Washington? After pondering for a while, Little Joseph told Grandpa that he had only heard of George Washington, the first president of the United States; but not anything about Booker T. Washington. So he asked Grandpa, Who is Booker T. Washington, and what does the middle initial T represent? Does the middle initial T represent Terry or Tommy? No son, replied Grandpa, the T does not represent Terry or Tommy. Booker Taliaferro Washington was his name and empowering African American students was his claim. Little Joseph asked Grandpa, can you tell me about Booker Taliaferro Washington? Well my boy, I'm glad you asked, said Grandpa! Booker Taliaferro Washington was born in the year 1856, which was a very long time ago. He was a slave on a small farm in Virginia. He moved with his family after the Emancipation Proclamation was signed and worked in the salt furnaces and coal mines of West Virginia.

The words Emancipation Proclamation had a lot of syllables and sounded very strange thought Little Joseph, so he asked Grandpa to tell him about it. Well, Little Joseph, the Emancipation Proclamation was a document signed by former president Abraham Lincoln that abolished slavery and freed all enslaved African Americans, and that's how Booker T. Washington gained his freedom. Booker T. Washington attended Hampton Institute where he studied law and the ministries and later became a teacher. Little Joseph said Booker T. Washington was a very smart man, and Grandpa agreed. Grandpa said he was so smart, that he developed and created a college in 1881 named Tuskegee Normal and Industrial Institute.

At Tuskegee Normal and Industrial Institute, Booker T. Washington taught students the importance of self-employment, land ownership, and business savvy skills. In 1895, Booker T. Washington made a powerful speech before the Cotton States Exposition called The Atlanta Compromise Address. Little Joseph asked Grandpa, is Booker T. Washington still alive?

No, said Grandpa, I'm sorry to say, Booker T. Washington died in 1915, but his accomplishments and heroics continue to live today. However, there is a school in Atlanta that's named after Booker T. Washington. Would you want to attend a school named after Booker T. Washington asked Grandpa? Sure I would exclaim Little Joseph! Maybe one day I could create and develop my own college just like Booker T. Washington created Tuskegee Normal and Industrial Institute. Maybe one day you will, responded Grandpa. Grandpa cleared his throat and reached for his raspberry lemonade, and then he stared up at the ceiling again. After some time passed, Little Joseph asked Grandpa, do you know any more stories about famous people in which the Atlanta schools are named? He also asked his Grandpa, was everything okay? You would tell me if something was wrong. Grandpa continued to stare up at the ceiling in silence.

Suddenly, he cleared his throat and asked Little Joseph if he had ever heard of Alonzo F. Herndon. He waited for a while fully knowing that Little Joseph didn't have a clue. In fact, Little Joseph had never heard anything on the radio or television concerning Alonzo F. Herndon. Well, let me see, replied Little Joseph, my second grade teacher's first name is Alonzo, but his last name is Bradley. Are you talking about Mr. Bradley, my second grade teacher? I'm not referring to Alonzo Bradley. I'm referring to Alonzo F. Herndon, replied Grandpa. Hey Grandpa, please tell me a story about Alonzo F. Herndon, asked Little Joseph? Grandpa cleared his throat and said, Alonzo Franklin Herndon was his name and innovative expertise in business was his claim. Alonzo Franklin Herndon was born a Georgia slave in 1858. Hey Grandpa, guess what, Alonzo Franklin Herndon and Booker Taliaferro Washington were both born in the 1850's and both men were enslaved. That's right, said Grandpa, I can see that you've been listening and paying close attention.

Hey Grandpa, when former president Lincoln signed the Emancipation Proclamation to free Booker Taliaferro Washington, did it also free Alonzo Franklin Herndon as well asked Little Joseph? It sure did, replied Grandpa! The Emancipation Proclamation not only freed Booker Taliaferro Washington and Alonzo Franklin Herndon, but the signed document also freed many enslaved African Americans. Little Joseph asked Grandpa, did Alonzo Franklin Herndon develop and create a college like Booker Taliaferro Washington? No replied Grandpa, however, Alonzo Franklin Herndon did create and develop one of Atlanta's finest barber shops. In fact, Alonzo F. Herndon owned and operated three barbershops, but the Crystal Palace was the prettiest and most stylish of them all. What was so stylish about the Crystal Palace asked Little Joseph? Alonzo F. Herndon's Crystal Palace Barbershop was designed with fashion and elegance. His barbershop had marble floors with a crystal chandelier hanging from the top of the ceiling. I think the crystal chandelier is where the name Crystal Palace originated from, said Grandpa. Alonzo F. Herndon invested the money he earned cutting hair into real estate. When Grandpa mentioned real estate, Little Joseph wasn't really sure what he was talking about. So Little Joseph asked, what is real estate?

Real estate is property in buildings and land, said Grandpa. So Alonzo F. Herndon purchased land, houses, and buildings with the money he earned from cutting hair, inquired Little Joseph. That's exactly what he did, said Grandpa. By the 1900's, Alonzo F. Herndon was one of the largest African American property owners in the city of Atlanta. Alonzo F. Herndon also started a business called Atlanta Life Insurance Company and was considered one of Atlanta's wealthiest African American men. Is Alonzo F. Herndon still alive asked little Joseph? No, said Grandpa, I'm sorry to say, Alonzo F. Herndon died in 1927, but his achievements and business innovations are still practiced and embraced by many people living today. However, there is a school in Atlanta that's named after Alonzo F. Herndon. Would you want to attend a school named after Alonzo F. Herndon asked Grandpa?

Sure I would, said little Joseph! Maybe one day, I could create and develop my own business just like Alonzo F. Herndon created the stylish Crystal Palace barbershop and The Atlanta Life Insurance Company. Maybe one day you will, said Grandpa. As Grandpa rocked in his old squeaky chair, with Little Joseph sitting in his lap, he continued to think of many other historically famous people in which the Atlanta schools are named. Meanwhile Grandpa cleared his throat and gulped down the remaining gulps of his raspberry lemonade, he asked little Joseph had he ever heard of Mary McLeod Bethune? This time, it was little Joseph who didn't say anything. After sitting in his grandfather's lap and listening to him tell his famous stories, little Joseph fell fast asleep.

14

The End

3R(Remember-Recognize-Recall) Resource Hub

The purpose of the 3R Resource Hub is to provide a fundamental approach of questioning through Remembering, Recognizing, & Recalling. This cognitive approach incorporates an instructional bank of inquiries that supports multiple academic disciplines transferable into authentic real-world problem solving.

GB 3rd-5th(Grade Band 3rd-5th) ELA (Content English Language Arts)

1. (GB-3ELA) Describe the part of speech in which the word rainy is used in this sentence: One rainy Saturday afternoon in Sacramento, California, Little Joseph and his Grandpa, gathered around the kitchen table for an afternoon snack.

   (GB-3ELA)Think about at least three alternate words for (rainy) that you as an author may have used?

2. (GB-4ELA) In the story, Little Joseph expressed that his Grandpa was the best storyteller in all of California. Provide at least two contextual clues from the story that would support Little Joseph's assessment of his Grandpa?

   (GB-4ELA) Identify some characteristics that you as an author would need to be considered a good storyteller?

3. (GB-5ELA) In the story, Grandpa talked about Booker T. Washington and Alonzo F. Herndon. Compare (Similar) and Contrast (Differences) individual characteristics of both men.

   (GB-5ELA) If you were the author of Grandpa's Stories, identify at least two people of interest that you would want to write about and why?

GB 3rd-5th(Grade Band 3rd-5th) Sci. (Content Science)

4. (GB-3Sci) Some examples of precipitation are hail, sleet, and snow. Illustrate the precipitation type that was identified in the story? Did the author indicate or provide any contextual clues in determining the magnitude or intensity of the precipitation?

5. (GB-4Sci) In the story, Grandpa talked about selling his tire company and moving to Atlanta. Considering that a tire is made in the shape of a circle, sketch and name at least 5 objects that's made like a circle?

6. (GB-5Sci) In the story, Grandpa mentioned Alonzo F Herndon's crystal chandelier hanging on the inside of his Barbershop. A crystal is a solid whose molecules (or atoms) are arranged in a repeating pattern. One example of a crystal is sugar, list at least 3 food items that contain natural sugars?

GB 3rd-5th(Grade Band 3rd-5th) Soc. (Content Social Studies)

7. (GB-3Soc) Some examples of the major United States oceans are Atlantic, Indian, Artic, and the Pacific as being the largest. Considering that Little Joseph and his Grandpa live in California, what major ocean borders the state where they currently reside? What major ocean borders the state where Little Joseph's new school is located?

8. (GB-4Soc) The Gold Rush (1848–1855) was a gold rush that began on January 24, 1848, when gold was found by James W. Marshall. As news spread of the discovery, did thousands of prospective gold miners travel by sea or over land to California or Georgia? Defend your position?

9. (GB-5Soc) President Abraham Lincoln issued the Emancipation Proclamation on January 1, 1863. The proclamation declared that all persons held as slaves within the rebellious states shall be free. If you were the 16th President of the United

States, would you have signed a proclamation to free all en-slaved people? Defend your position?

GB 3rd-5th(Grade Band 3rd-5th) Math. (Content Mathematics)

10. (GB-3Math) In the story, Grandpa expressed that Booker Tal-iaferro Washington was born in the year 1856. The number 1856 is a four digit number, identify digit that's in the ones, tens, hundreds, and thousands place?

11. (GB-4Math) In the story, Grandpa mentioned that Alonzo Franklin Herndon was born a Georgia slave in 1858 and died in the year 1927. Calculate the lifespan of Alonzo Franklin Herndon, take the difference and multiply it by 3, finally, take the product and divide it by 3. Does the quotient equals a number divisible by 3?

12. (GB-5Math) One of Grandpa's favorite lunch items during story time was chocolate chip cookies. Considering that Choc-olate Chip Cookies are shaped like a circle. Let's imagine that Grandpa cut one cookie into 8 pieces. He gave 2 pieces to Little Joseph, he ate 3 pieces, and saved 3 pieces. What fraction rep-resents the number of pieces of cookies did Grandpa save? Now subtract 1/4 from the answer, and then convert it to a decimal?

"Grandpa's Famous Stories is an awesome story that rejuvenates self-awareness, ruminates on past accomplishments, and resonates the heart."

Dr. Craig L. Oliver Sr. | Senior Pastor of Elizabeth Baptist Church in Atlanta, GA | General Overseer of FGBCF | Author of Travel Lightly

"Grandpa's Famous Stories explores the possibilities of HOPE and uncovers a foundation of rich tradition for children of all ages to emulate."

Dr. Evelyn J. Mobley | Principal of Phoenix Academy (Atlanta Public Schools) | Georgia Association for Alternative Education 2017-2018 Administrator of the Year

"Grandpa's Famous Stories truly inspires the heroic accomplishments of the past and encourages one to reach beyond the walls of mediocrity."

Dr. E. Dewey Smith | Senior Pastor of The House of Hope Atlanta and The House of Hope Macon | Author of A God Dream

"Grandpa's Famous Stories unlocks the prospects of self-complacency and encourages an atmosphere of deliberate diligence."

John Herring | Senior Pastor of Glorious Hope Baptist Church in Macon, GA

Have you ever wondered what it would be like to interact with some of the great American innovative pioneers of the past? People like Booker T. Washington, Alonzo F. Herndon, even Mary McLeod Bethune. Could you imagine walking side by side with them as they blaze the trail of Greatness? Let's take a journey with Grandpa as he shares his famous stories with his favorite grandson, Little Joseph. Little Joseph considers his Grandpa as the Best storyteller in all of California. Some even consider Grandpa as, The Greatest of all Time. Grandpa's Famous Stories will allow you to explore the rich history and accomplishments of our notable American entrepreneurs. Grandpa's Famous Stories will ultimately inspire you to self-reflect and ponder the potential and innovative possibilities that live within you.

About the Author

Author Dr. Cedrick Gilbert is a native of Atlanta GA. He's a graduate of Henry McNeal Turner High School and Morris Brown College. He started his career as an educator in 1997 with the Atlanta Public School System as an elementary school teacher. He has earned a Masters of Arts in Education with majors in Educational Curriculum and Technology from the University of Phoenix. He has also earned a Ph.D. in Educational Leadership with a concentration in E-Learning from TUI University. In addition, he's facilitated graduate level courses as an Adjunct Professor with Argosy University, Columbia Southern University, TUI University, Concordia University, Ashford University, and Central Michigan University. He has earned membership with Atlanta Association of Educators, Georgia Association of Educators, National Educators Association, ASCD, and The National Council of Teachers of Mathematics. He is also the founder and chief executive operator of Once Upon A Time Productions, LLC. Arthur Dr. Cedrick Gilbert is very passionate about positively impacting the lives of children and he believes that "A finisher isn't afraid to fail; however, a failure is reluctant to finish"